READY, SET, *Write!*

Creative Ideas to Get Kids Writing

Debra Kuzbik

PEGUIS PUBLISHERS

WINNIPEG • MANITOBA • CANADA

Printed and bound in Canada by Hignell Printing Limited

96 97 98 99 00 5 4 3 2 1

Canadian Cataloguing in Publication Data

Kuzbik, Debra, 1953–

    Ready, set, write!

    Includes bibliographical references.
    ISBN 1-895411-84-X

1. English language - Composition and exercises - Study and teaching (Primary). I. Title.

LB1576.K89 1996   372.6'23044   C96-920079-X

Cover design: Bill Stewart
Book design: In house

Peguis Publishers
100-318 McDermot Avenue
Winnipeg, Manitoba
Canada R3A 0A2
1-800-667-9673

This book is dedicated to the young authors
whose creativity, imagination, and effort
reflect the wonder, hope, and joy of childhood.

Contents

Introduction

Children are born communicators—from that first lusty, newborn cry to the first word to an overjoyed, "I can read! I can read!" Children are naturally curious about language and it's only a matter of time until speaking and listening progress to interest in reading and writing.

There are four basic language processes: speaking, listening, reading, and writing. Cambourne (1988) shows that children acquire language skills in a holistic and integrated fashion; when planning language activities for children, it is important to integrate all four processes. Although this book focuses mainly on writing, the activities in Part II incorporate the other three language processes— reading, listening, and speaking—through editing, publishing, and sharing student writing and children's literature.

HOW AND WHEN TO USE THIS BOOK

Daily writing is considered an integral part of whole-language instruction. Writing experiences may take the form of journal writing, sustained silent writing (SSW), or writer's workshop. For many students, especially those with a broad range of background experiences, inspiration comes easily. For others, however, daily writing is an exercise in frustration and boredom. Often students need a catalyst, a spark, something to jiggle the imagination.

The activities in *Ready, Set, Write!* are designed to be completed in thirty minutes. The amount of time spent on prewriting activities, such as questioning, discussing, webbing, and brainstorming, will be determined by the needs of the students. Beginning writers may need a lot of direction from the teacher. Developing writers may require only a short discussion prior to writing.

Ready, Set, Write! is teacher-friendly. You are encouraged to modify, adapt, and expand the activities to suit your needs and the needs of your students. Some teachers may find that the book is most useful at the beginning of the school year when students need more guidance and direction in their writing. Others may want to use it once a week or alternate the activities with self-chosen writing topics. Still others may continue to use it daily with some children and allow more advanced writers to choose their own topics.

The activities are open-ended. Each allows you the flexibility to keep in mind the varying skill levels of students. Younger, beginning writers may express themselves through pictures or a combination of pictures and words or dictated stories. Developing writers may write a few sentences or several pages.

THE READING CONNECTION

Many of the writing activities are linked to works by children's authors. Children's literature is important because it teaches children about the world and their place in it. By linking children's literature to writing activities, your students will begin to see themselves as authors who have something important to say. Use these books as a springboard for writing, a model for students to follow, or as a culminating activity at the end of the writing session.

PART I

Organizing and Managing Writing

DAILY WRITING

In an age in which we can connect with people on the other side of the planet at the touch of a keystroke, effective written communication is more important than ever. As teachers, it is our responsibility to teach children how to communicate not only clearly, but eloquently and imaginatively as well. One way is through writing, which, like all skills, improves with practice. We know that children learn best by doing and that frequent writing experiences both improve writing fluency and proficiency and help children understand the patterns, power, and beauty of language. As well, giving children daily opportunities to write helps them shape, organize, and express their ideas and become critical and creative thinkers. As their writing skills improve and their knowledge and experiences expand, they develop an appreciation for effective and controlled use of language.

MAKING TIME TO WRITE

To improve writing fluency and proficiency, Graves (1983) recommends that primary students write for at least twenty minutes each day. You can increase that time, depending on the ability and grade level of your students. Some teachers like to start the school day with a writing activity while others prefer to conclude the language arts time-block with writing. Just be sure your students view writing not as a separate entity, but as an integral part of the other language processes—reading, speaking, and listening. You'll find many opportunities during the school day to integrate writing into other subject areas. You can have students:

- write letters to their favorite authors

- write invitations to parents and special guests and thank-you letters to parent volunteers and classroom visitors

- use their art as a springboard for story writing and poetry

- write song lyrics to use with familiar tunes

- write reports about animals, countries, other cultures, nutrition, or other topics you are studying in science, social studies, or health

- record observations. For example, during a study of winter, students might describe the texture and appearance of the snow: Is it crusty? Is it soft and fluffy? Does it sparkle? Does it crunch when you walk on it?

After viewing films or videos, younger students can write about one new thing they learned. Older students could summarize the contents.

🖋 keep a math journal. Start each math lesson with a problem of the day. Make these real-life and relevant. For example: Mrs. Jones has brought two pans of brownies to class. There are twenty-five students in our class. How can we divide the brownies equally? Have the students illustrate the problem, then explain how they would solve it. This activity gives students the opportunity to practice logical and creative problem solving, and gives you a window into each child's thought processes.

🖋 outline experiments they have conducted in science. Students could design an experiment to see how long it takes snow to melt: Collect several small containers of snow. Place them in different areas of the classroom, such as on a window ledge, near a heat source, and in a cupboard. Have the students write out the steps of the experiment, record when they think the snow in each container will melt, and tell why they came to that conclusion. After the snow has melted ask the students to write what they have learned from the experiment.

🖋 write letters requesting information on topics of study. For example, if students are studying cities of Canada, they could write to various Chambers of Commerce for information about the city they are learning about. Government departments and embassies of foreign countries will also send information upon request.

EDITING AND PUBLISHING

It is not necessary, or even desirable, to have students publish every piece of writing they do. Nor should they be expected to complete every piece they start—young children can get side-tracked easily. If they keep all rough drafts, they may return to an unfinished piece later. As long as they are writing each day, their writing skills and fluency will continue to improve.

It is a good idea, however, to have students publish one piece of writing every week or two. By publishing their work, students learn about the process of writing and how to prepare their work for an audience. You may want to designate one particular day to be "publishing day" or you may assign your students a certain number of stories to be published in a month. Students who have problems completing a piece of writing may need extra attention. The difficulty usually lies in the mechanics of writing, not a child's lack of story ideas. Children who are reluctant writers often have not developed the fine muscle control necessary to put ideas down on paper before they are lost. One way to help is to scribe for them. Ask the child to dictate a story to you. If necessary, prompt with questions such as "What will happen if...?" and "What will happen next?"

THE WRITING PROCESS

The writing process can be broken down into four steps: prewriting, drafting, editing and revising, and publishing. Teach each step to the students and post the process at your writing center.

1. PREWRITING: LOOKING FOR GEMS

At this stage, students plan the writing and, depending on the purpose of the writing and the intended audience, decide what form it will take. They might

- collect words and ideas
- brainstorm
- listen to a story or music
- discuss
- web an idea
- watch a video
- draw a picture, storyboard, or story map
- develop a list of questions

2. DRAFTING: FINDING THE GEMS

When writing the rough draft, it is important to let the ideas flow. Encourage students to write quickly so that they do not lose any ideas. Giving students a time limit will help them overcome the need to edit as they write. Capitalization, punctuation, and spelling are not important at this time. One useful strategy is to have students circle any words they think they've misspelled, then return to check these words later during editing.

3. EDITING AND REVISING: POLISHING THE GEMS

Teach students a couple of simple strategies they can use to edit their writing. (At this stage in the writing process, many students may lose interest in the story or be dissatisfied with how it turned out. Sometimes setting a story aside for a few days is all that is necessary to renew interest.)

ORAL EDITING

Arrange students in groups of four to six. Have each group member read his or her rough draft to the group. Ask the others to tell what they liked best about the draft and to give one suggestion for improving it. Remind students that only positive comments are acceptable.

Using the oral editing strategy, Henry, a grade-three student, reads his rough draft to classmates.

CALL IN THE C.O.P.S.!

Each letter represents one element of writing mechanics:

C—Capitalization

O—Overall Editing

- Does each sentence make sense?

- Can I improve my word pictures by adding descriptive words, phrases, or details?

P—Punctuation

S—Spelling

Natasha, a grade-two student, is reading her story to herself to make sure each sentence makes sense—the "O" step in the C.O.P.S. strategy to editing.

PARTNER EDITING

Have each student trade the rough draft of a story with a partner and edit the work with colored pencil crayons. Post a color-coded editing model for them to follow. For example:

red circle—capitalization mistake

two green lines—punctuation mistake

blue box—spelling error

orange question mark over a sentence—meaning is unclear

purple caret (^)—a word has been left out

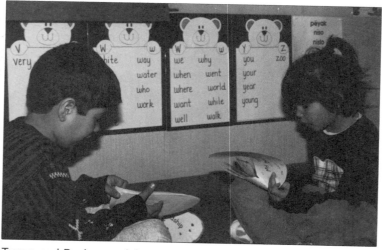

Tyson and Becky are doing a partner edit—sharing their stories with each other.

OVERHEAD EDITING

Make an overhead transparency of a different student's journal story each day. Practice editing the work together. Some students may wish to remain anonymous while others will happily incorporate the suggestions of classmates into their writing.

SELF-EDITING

Develop a checklist that students can use to edit their own work. The checklist can be changed as students' writing skills grow and develop. It might include the following directives:

- Each sentence begins with a capital letter.

- Names of people and places begin with a capital letter.

- Each sentence ends with a punctuation mark.

- There are quotation marks around spoken words.

- I have checked the spelling of any words I did not know.

- Each sentence makes sense.

- My story has a beginning, middle, and end.

- It is written carefully and neatly.

4. PUBLISHING: DISPLAYING THE GEMS

There are countless ways to publish students' writing. By varying how they publish their stories, you are more likely to keep your students' interest and motivation high. Here are some suggestions.

- Enlist parent volunteers to input students' work on a computer.

- Make booklets with construction paper or wallpaper covers. Keep a supply of these booklets on hand at your writing center or have the students make them as needed.

- Make big books.

- Make books in the shape of the topic.

- Make pop-up books.

- Coil-bind a collection of stories or poetry into a class book.

- Photocopy a supply of each students' class picture. Store these in a personalized envelope at your writing center. Just before a student publishes a book, he or she can write a short biography to accompany the picture and attach both to the back cover of the book.

MANAGING THE PAPER EXPLOSION

Help students keep track of their idea lists, rough drafts, works in progress, and published works. One simple way is to give each student a writing portfolio. You can turn an ordinary file folder into a writing portfolio by folding and stapling the bottom to make a pocket. Or you can buy writing portfolios wherever teacher supplies are sold. Use one side of the portfolio to hold story ideas, brainstormed lists of words, story webs, and so on, and the other side to store the writing journal. Encourage the students to jot down story ideas and interesting words as they come across them and store these in their portfolios. Have them do all their rough drafts in their journal and get them into the habit of labeling and dating everything.

At the end of each writing session, collect the portfolios and store them in a tote box or photocopy-paper box. If your students work in groups, give each group its own storage box—word lists and story ideas can easily get lost in students' desks or fall out of the writing portfolio. Teach the students to file the portfolios right-side up!

Pizza boxes make great portfolios for published work. They are inexpensive and available from any pizza parlor. Share the portfolio contents with parents during conferences; at the end of the school year, each student will have a cherished keepsake.

SHARING PUBLISHED STORIES: DISPLAYING THE GEMS

Although publishing is the final stage of the writing process, don't file the work away in the portfolio or send it home with the students just yet. Because all writing is done with an audience in mind, it is important that you give students the opportunity to share their published work. Once again, variety is the key—schedule regular, varied sharing opportunities. You may want to try some of the following:

- Author's Chair—Designate your chair or a special stool as the Author's Chair. Once a week, have one group of students share their published work with the rest of the class from the Author's Chair. Teach the students what is expected of a good audience: listen quietly and attentively, show appreciation by clapping, and make positive comments about the student author's work.

- Invite another class to listen to your students' published work.

- Arrange to have your students read several published works at a school assembly.

- Take your students' published work on the road! Arrange to have them read to seniors in a nursing home or to preschoolers at a day care center.

- Invite parents to an afternoon poetry party or story soirée. Serve refreshments afterwards.

- Display published poetry on classroom or hallway bulletin boards.

- Include several published stories in the monthly school newsletter.

- Arrange a display of student writing at a local shopping mall.

- When your students have published a large number of story booklets, invite a younger class to borrow from your student library.

- Videotape students reading their published work. Let each student take the videotape home one evening to share with his or her family.

- Tape-record spooky Halloween stories complete with sound effects. Send the audiotape home with each student.

- Each month, arrange for a group of students to share published stories with the school principal or vice-principal in his or her office.

- Establish a classroom writer's club. Each month publish a collection of student writing. Send one copy of the collection home with each student and sell additional copies to teachers and students in other classrooms to offset the cost of photocopying.

- Invite the local newspaper to feature student writing once a month.

- Plan a special year-end celebration of writing.

✎ Have each student choose two or three favorite published pieces from the school year and invite parents to an evening of readings. Plan to have parent volunteers bring refreshments (six dainties could be the price of admission!). To make the evening extra-special, hold the event at a local restaurant, art gallery, or library.

EVALUATION: MONITORING STUDENT GROWTH IN WRITING

To monitor student growth in writing, you need to have a beginning-of-the-year benchmark. One of the easiest ways to evaluate students' writing is to have them write you a letter on the first day of school. (If students are not yet reading or writing, you could ask them simply to print their name. From it you will be able to assess letter formation, and whether they can differentiate between uppercase and lowercase letters.)

First, give each student an envelope containing a letter from you. In it, tell about your family and hobbies; favorite food, color, animal, and number; places you've visited; and plans you have for the future. Invite the students to write back to you telling about their families, their hobbies, what they like best about school, and things they would like to learn about this year. Assess the letters using a writing skills checklist (see appendix, page 85). File them and compare with writing samples throughout the year. At the end of the year, return the

Grade-three students sharing published work. (Top) Larissa is reading at a class "publishing party." (Bottom) Natasha and Cedar are reading published poetry.

letters to the students. They will be amazed at how much their writing has improved!

The writing journal is another useful tool for assessment. Choose one day each month to photocopy each student's journal entry. Evaluate each month's sample according to a skills checklist (see appendix, page 85). File the samples with the beginning-of-the-year letter.

Finally, evaluate each student's portfolio of published work. Give the students an opportunity to assess the contents of their own portfolios through writing conferences. Ask the students to select three or four of their strongest published pieces for assessment. Sample conference questions might include:

- What do you think is the best part of this work?

- Can you identify the beginning, middle, and end of this piece?

- What message does this piece communicate?

- Do you think readers will enjoy this piece? Why or why not?

- What kinds of writing do you like best?

- What kinds of writing are most difficult for you?

- When you encounter difficulties in writing, what do you do?

- How is this piece better than others you have written?

- How could you improve your next piece of writing?

PART II

A Treasury of Writing Activities

1. I WISH I MAY, I WISH I MIGHT

Have students brainstorm a list of stories in which wishes are granted (for example, *Cinderella, The Fisherman and His Wife, Aladdin,* and *The Tinder Box*). Discuss what the characters in these stories wish for and what happens after the wishes are granted. Ask the students what they might wish for and what might happen to them after the wish is granted. Then invite them to choose a story starter from the following list or make up one of their own:

- If I could have three wishes...
- I wish I could go...
- My wish for the world is...
- I wish I could make...
- My wish for my best friend is...
- My wish for my family is...

SUGGESTED READING

Big Anthony and the Magic Ring by Tomie dePaola
Strega Nona by Tomie dePaola
Three Wishes by Lucille Clifton

2. WHAT GOOD ARE MITTENS?

Bring in a mitten from your school lost-and-found box or borrow one from a student. Brainstorm things the mitten could be used for. List these on the chalkboard or chart paper. Who could wear it? Who could live in it? What could it keep warm besides your hand?

Ask the students to write a story about an unusual use for the mitten.

SUGGESTED READING

The Mitten by Jan Brett

3. STORY RECIPES

Give each student a recipe file card. Have them think up four to six story "ingredients"; for example:

25 strawberries	1 boy
5 angry bees	1 hot air balloon

Collect the cards and randomly redistribute them to the students. Have them cook up a delicious story!

SUGGESTED READING

Stone Soup by John Stewig

The Wolf's Chicken Stew by Keiko Kasza

4. JUST PRETENDS

List the following story starters on a chart posted at your writing center or record them on a laminated card for students to refer to when looking for new story ideas.

Pretend

- you are a dust cloth for dusting furniture.

- you are a lollipop being eaten.

- you have chocolate instead of blood in your veins.

- you are a turtle who can't get back into your shell.

- you are a computer with a virus.

- you can shrink or grow to any size you want.

- you can run, skate, or swim faster than anyone else.

- a leprechaun has just led you to a pot of gold.

- a genie has granted you three wishes.

- you have the power to cast one spell.

5. CUTOUTS I

Have the students each cut out three unrelated magazine pictures. Collect them, mix them up, and randomly distribute three pictures to each student. Then ask each student to create a story about the three pictures.

6. CUTOUTS II

Ask students to bring in old magazines and calendars. Then start a file collection of pictures of settings and characters. Students can refer to the files when they need an idea, and add interesting pictures that they find to the collection.

7. CUTOUTS III

Cut and laminate scenic pictures from old calendars. Invite your students to "go for a walk" through the pictures and describe what they see. Ask them to use their imaginations to describe the sounds and smells they might experience there.

8. A JUICY POEM

Bring a large watermelon to class. As you slice it up, have the students brainstorm words and phrases to describe its size, color, texture, and appearance. Have a student record these on the chalkboard or chart paper. Give each student a piece of watermelon to enjoy as he or she writes a poem describing its sensations.

9. A RUNNING ADVENTURE

Find the oldest, most worn-out, running shoe in your school lost-and-found box. Tuck the following note inside the runner or tie it to the shoelace:

Help! I'm lost! Please help me find my twin. You wouldn't believe what I've been through.

Ask the students

- Where has the shoe been?
- How can we help it?
- What has happened to its "twin"?
- Who does it belong to?

Have the students write an adventure story about the shoe's travels.

10. WHO AM I?

This activity will help your students improve their descriptive writing. Write each student's name on a slip of paper. Let them take turns selecting a name out of a jar or basket. Have the students do one of the following:

- Describe what the person looks like.
- Describe one feature, such as the hands or hair, of that person.
- Describe what the person is good at.
- Describe what you like best about the person.

Remind students that only positive descriptions are acceptable. Have students share their writings aloud and have everyone else try to guess who is being described.

11. LET'S TALK!

Have the students bring a favorite doll or teddy bear to school. Ask them to write a conversation they would like to have with it if it could talk, or have them write a conversation with a friend's doll or teddy bear. The students could write their conversations as a cartoon strip, in dialogue balloons, or they could practice using quotation marks.

12. WHAT AM I?

This activity is similar to "Who Am I?" (page 26). This time, ask the students to each choose one object in the classroom and observe it silently for a minute or two. Ask them to think about its color, size, shape, and texture and then write a detailed description of the object without actually naming it. Students will enjoy guessing what each object is.

What am I?

I have letters all over me.
I am round and I have water
on me and at night stars came.
around me.
        What am I?
        (the globe)

"What Am I?"
by Kenny, age 9

13. WE ARE POWERLESS!

Ask your students what they think would happen if all the electrical power in the world was suddenly shut off. Brainstorm a list of things that would no longer work. Ask them to write a story about the day there was no power. How will power be restored?

14. WHAT'S THE *REAL* STORY?

Brainstorm a list of familiar fairy tales. Ask each student to choose one of the fairy tales and rewrite it from another character's point of view. For example:

- *Hansel and Gretel*, as told by the witch
- *Cinderella*, as told by the wicked stepmother
- *Snow White and the Seven Dwarfs*, as told by Doc
- *Jack and the Beanstalk*, as told by the giant
- *Little Red Riding Hood*, as told by the wolf

SUGGESTED READING

The True Story of the Three Little Pigs by Jon Scieszka

15. FLYING HIGH

We've all read about flying carpets in stories. Ask your students: What would it be like if your bike could fly? How about your skateboard [or runners or Rollerblades]? Where would you go? What would it be like up in the clouds? Write about your adventures.

SUGGESTED READING

The Wreck of the Zephyr by Chris Van Allsburg

16. CLOTHES ENCOUNTER

Ask students to think about a favorite outfit. It might be one they wear now, or an outfit they have outgrown. Have them close their eyes to picture every detail and then write a description of it. Ask them to tell why they like it so much. Is it something they would wear on a special occasion? Alternately, students could describe an outfit they dislike or imagine one they wish they could have.

SUGGESTED READING

Thomas' Snowsuit by Robert Munsch

The Principal's New Clothes by Stephanie Calmenson

The Queen Who Stole the Sky by Jennifer Garrett

The Purple Coat by Amy Hest

17. SWEET DREAMS

Dreams can be silly, funny, or scary. Tell the students about a dream you've had. Ask them to think about a dream they can remember, then to pretend that the dream came true. Have them write about it.

SUGGESTED READING

The Sweetest Fig by Chris Van Allsburg

18. WHAT IF?

Hang story ideas from a "writing tree"—a small tree branch secured in a pail of sand or plaster of Paris. Write a "What if" on a small piece of construction paper, attach some string or wool, and hang it from a branch of the writing tree. Ideas could be changed monthly, reflecting seasonal topics. For example, autumn topics could be written on leaf-shaped paper, Halloween story ideas on pumpkins, and winter themes on snowballs. Here are some suggestions to get you started.

- What if it snowed marshmallows?
- What if it rained chocolate milk?
- What if your hair turned pink?
- What if you found a book of magic spells?
- What if you met an alien from outer space?
- What if your dog started talking?
- What if the sky turned green?
- What if you found a little door on the trunk of a tree?
- What if you could be principal for a day?
- What if you could be any other person for a day?

SUGGESTED READING

If I Were a Penguin by Heidi Goennel

What If It Snowed Marshmallows
It was a cold windy day
and it started to snow.
Peter, a little boy, looked
out the window again and
saw marshmallows falling from
from the sky. So he ran
outside and was picking them
up and eating them. His mom
saw and came running out,
the mom and Peter gathered
up marshmallows and made
rice crispy cake and ate some
pieces of it as Peter fell asleep
it stopped snowing marshmallows
The end.

"What If It Snowed Marshmallows" by Tiffany, age 8

19. MY FAVORITE MONSTER

Ask each student to create a character web for his or her new pet—a monster! Use the web to describe what the monster looks like, what it eats, its habits, and its traits. Have them use the information from the web to write a story about the new pet monster.

SUGGESTED READING

The Very Worst Monster by Pat Hutchins

20. WHAT HOLDS UP THE MOON?

Years ago people did not know how the moon stayed up in the sky. Was it glued in place? Did it follow a path in the sky?

Read *Min-Yo and the Moon Dragon* by Elizabeth Hillman to find out what happens when the moon begins to slowly fall toward the earth. Then have students write their own story about how the moon stays up in the sky.

SUGGESTED READING

What Holds Up the Moon? by Lois Simmie

21. WHAT GOOD IS A PAPER BAG?

Bring a variety of paper bags to class. Ask the students to brainstorm a list of uses for the paper bags. Encourage them to think creatively—the wilder the better! For example, a paper bag could be made into a mask or a puppet, used to start a fire if you're lost in the woods, made into wrapping paper, or used as drawing paper. Have the students either choose one use from the list or devise a new use and write a story about the day they had to depend on a paper bag.

SUGGESTED READING

The Paper Bag Princess by Robert Munsch

22. DOES IT GROW ON A TREE?

Brainstorm a list of things that grow on trees. Then ask the students to come up with another list—things that couldn't possibly grow on trees, or could they? The list might include:

chocolate bars	watermelons
ice-cream cones	comic books
cupcakes	magic wands
baseball caps	diamonds
icicles	running shoes

Have the students draw a picture of the magical tree that grows in their yard and then write a story about it.

SUGGESTED READING

The Balloon Tree by Phoebe Gilman

23. OUR MASCOT'S ADVENTURES

Early in the school year, bring a stuffed animal to class. Tell the students it will be your class mascot for the year and invite them to come up with a name for it. Make a class booklet that includes a cover page and one blank page for each student. Keep your mascot and the booklet at the writing center and encourage the students to each write one adventure for the mascot. Send the completed booklet and mascot home with each child for an evening.

24. MAGIC TOOLS

Display a variety of objects such as pens, pencils, paintbrushes, chalk, paper clips, and rulers. Tell the students that each object has one magical quality. Ask them to choose one of the objects and write a story about it and its magical ability.

SUGGESTED READING

The Magic Paintbrush by Robin Muller

Liang and the Magic Paintbrush by Demi

25. WORDLESS BOOKS? NOT FOR LONG!

Collect a variety of wordless picture books from your school or public library. Have the students work with a partner to write a story to go with the illustrations. Display the library book together with the student-written story at your reading center.

Students might like to make their own wordless picture books and then exchange these with a partner to write the text.

Look for the following authors of wordless books:

Mitsumasa Anno   Frank Asch

John Goodall   Arnold Loebel

Tana Hoban   Mercer Mayer

Alexandra Day   Peter Spier

26. THE DAY THE ANIMALS WENT ON STRIKE

Ask your students: What would happen if all the animals decided to go on strike? Have the students choose an animal from the list or think of another one and write about it.

- the cow who wouldn't give milk
- the sheep who wouldn't give wool
- the bee who wouldn't make honey
- the beaver who wouldn't build a dam
- the skunk who wouldn't make a stink

SUGGESTED READING

Amos's Sweater by Janet Lunn

27. E.T. AND ME!

Tell your students: Pretend aliens from outer space have landed on Earth. You are the first person they encounter. What do they look like? How did they get here? What are they wearing? Where did they come from? What do they eat? What do you say to each other? Write an account of your encounter.

SUGGESTED READING

June 29,1999 by David Wiesner

28. WHAT DOES A DRAGON LOOK LIKE?

Ask the students to describe a dragon to someone who has never heard of dragons before. Have them close their eyes so that they can see the dragon clearly. Remember to describe its size, color, face, body, feet, wings, tail, skin, and special powers (such as breathing fire and flying). After they write a description, have them draw a picture of a dragon.

SUGGESTED READING

Everyone Knows What a Dragon Looks Like by Jay Williams

29. WORDS, WORDS, WORDS!

Start a collection of interesting and unusual words. Have each student choose five to include in a story. Ask them to look up any words they are unfamiliar with before starting to write. Students can contribute new words to the collection. Following are some words to start the collection:

mango	whimsical	platypus
meander	artichoke	guffaw
talons	amble	silo
quark	adobe	sycamore
trapeze	derelict	tuba

30. STORY STARTERS I

Story starters can be written on strips of paper and put into a jar or basket. Let students pick a story starter from the jar, and write about it. Here are some suggestions.

- I had just closed my eyes when...

- As I turned the corner I saw...

- I was watching the thunderstorm out the window when suddenly...

- When I got a breakaway in the last minute of the game...

- As I rode my bike along the bumpy path, I suddenly...

- The little purple man looked up at me and said...

- Just as I reached to pick up the glittering stone...

- When I opened the jar of peanut butter out popped...

- As I walked through the abandoned house, I suddenly heard...

- "You may have one wish," said the strange old woman, "But remember..."

31. RAINBOW RHYMES

Brainstorm a list of unusual colors with the students. A good source is the color names of crayons and pencil crayons. The list might include

sepia	cyan	magenta
aqua	saffron	cerise
chartreuse	mauve	violet
scarlet	crimson	sienna
emerald	ecru	sapphire

Let each student select a color and make a list of all the ideas that color brings to mind. Have them include feelings, smells, and sounds, as well as objects. Write the collection of ideas as a poem.

SUGGESTED READING

Hailstones and Halibut Bones by Mary O'Neill

"Orange is..."
by Paul, age 8

> Orange is...
> Orange is a nice
> juicy fruit,
> A very very, wiled
> suit.
> Orange is a
> flash of light, that's
> really quite bright.
> Orange is a lepord
> Or the colour of
> of a shepord's
> bright flowing hair

32. PLOT IT!

Make a collection of story characters and story settings. Write each on a slip of paper or file card and store in an envelope or recipe box. Have each student choose one or more characters and a setting and then make up a story plot. The students can add new characters and settings to the collection.

Character	Setting
an ugly giant	a rickety bridge
a kind witch	a haunted castle
a scarecrow	a spooky forest
a friendly ghost	a wishing well
a family of trolls	an attic
a fairy godmother	a cave
a beautiful princess	a cottage by the ocean
an angry queen	a jungle island
a leprechaun	a snow-covered mountain
a blind wizard	an oasis in the desert

33. EXTRA! EXTRA! READ ALL ABOUT IT!

Have the students cut out interesting newspaper headlines to use as story titles. Store these in a file folder or large envelope. Later, let each student select one headline and write about it. Have students update the collection occasionally. Newspaper photographs may also be collected. Have students cut off the captions before adding the pictures to the collection.

34. THE FORTUNE TELLER

Make a paper fan or finger fortune teller (the kind with the lift-up flaps that are labeled with colors and numbers). Let the students ask you questions about the future, which you "magically" answer with the help of your fortune teller. Then have the students pretend that they can tell the future. Ask them to think of a magical object that gives them the power to see the future. It might be a crystal ball, a magic gem, or wand. Have them write a story about a day in the life of a fortune teller.

SUGGESTED READING

The Magic Fan by Keith Baker
The Fortune-Tellers by Lloyd Alexander

35. YOUR WISH IS MY COMMAND

Cover an empty dish-soap bottle or other bottle with an interesting shape with wallpaper or self-sticking shelf paper. Ask the students to imagine that a genie lives in the bottle. Tell them that if the bottle is rubbed the genie will appear and grant a wish. Have them to write a story about the genie, being sure to describe what he or she looks like and telling what their wish is.

SUGGESTED READING

Aladdin and the Wonderful Lamp by Carol Carrick

The Toothpaste Genie by Frances Duncan

36. DESCRIBE IT!

Ask each student to write a description of his or her jacket. Remind them to describe the shape, texture, and decorative details as well as the style and color. Collect the descriptions and randomly distribute them to the students. Ask the students to draw the jacket based on the description they have received. Display the illustrations and have each student try to identify his or her jacket. Alternately, the students could describe their homes, runners, backpacks, or T-shirts.

37. MY FRIEND, THE TREE

Take your class on a walk to a nearby tree or trees. Tell the students they're going to "adopt" a tree. Ask them to think of words to describe the look, feel, and smell of the tree. Have them sketch the tree, and look closely for creatures that live in or on the tree. Have them "listen" to the tree while it tells its story. Ask them to write the story of the tree. Encourage them to visit the tree periodically to note the changes from season to season. Perhaps the tree has more than one story to tell!

SUGGESTED READING

Hello, Tree! by Joanne Ryder

Hurricane by David Wiesner

The Giving Tree by Shel Silverstein

38. EVERYBODY NEEDS SOMETHING!

In *Everybody Needs a Rock*, Byrd Baylor outlines a list of ten rules for finding the perfect rock. Read the book to the students and then ask them to create a similar story about another object such as a leaf, pine cone, feather, or cloud. Have them create their own list of rules for finding the perfect object.

39. SOMETHING FROM NOTHING

Ask the students to bring their favorite baby blanket to school (if they still have them!) How could the blankets be reused or recycled? Brainstorm a list of uses for these old, but much loved blankets. Ask the students to write about a new use for an old blanket or have each student write a story about his or her blanket and why it was (and perhaps still is) so special. Display the published stories with the owner's blanket.

SUGGESTED READING

Something From Nothing by Phoebe Gilman

Anna Marie's Blanket by Joanne Barkan

The Keeping Quilt by Patricia Polacco

The Patchwork Quilt by Valerie Flournoy

40. WHAT HAPPENS NEXT?

Read the students a familiar fairy tale such as *Sleeping Beauty* or *Hansel and Gretel*. Ask them to think about what happened after "happily ever after." Did Sleeping Beauty ever return to her parent's castle? Did Hansel and Gretel's father ever marry again? Ask the students to choose a fairy tale and write another chapter to the story.

SUGGESTED READING

The Frog Prince, Continued by Jon Scieszka

41. ALICE'S ADVENTURES

Read *The Third-Story Cat* by Leslie Baker to the students. It tells the story of a curious cat named Alice who lives in an apartment and longs to explore the park across the street. One day, when a window is left open, Alice gets her chance. After you have read the story ask the students to write another adventure for Alice. Where else would she like to explore? What dangers should she be aware of? How can she get back home? After the students have written their stories, read Baker's sequel, *The Antique Store Cat*. Once Alice gets outside, she is rescued from a rainstorm by a kindly antique store owner.

42. MY WEIRD AND WONDERFUL INVENTION

Ask the students to describe a chore or job they hate doing. Then have them invent a machine that will do the job for them. What is the invention called? How does it work? What does it do? What does it look like?

SUGGESTED READING

Clean Your Room, Harvey Moon! by Pat Cummings

43. "HOW TO" STORIES

Ask the students to describe a process; for example, how to make breakfast or how to ride a bike. Record the steps on the chalkboard or chart paper, making sure that they are in the correct order. Remind the students not to leave out any steps. Then have them either pick a topic from the following list or make up their own as the basis for a "how to" story:

- how to learn to like taking out the garbage

- how to eat a taco

- how to swat a mosquito in the dark

- how to make a snack in the middle of the night

- how to keep a frog as a pet without Mom finding out

SUGGESTED READING

How to Eat Fried Worms by Thomas Rockwell

Giting my ears perst
At frst they put on a
cotinbol. Then they mac
a little dot. Then they
put a neetl in yowr
ers. Then the i rings
are in.

"Getting My
Ears Pierced"
by Karen, age 6

44. SET IT UP!

Brainstorm a list of settings under the headings "when" and "where." Have each students choose one setting from the "when" list and one from the "where" list. Ask the students to create a story using the setting elements they have chosen. Here are some suggestions.

When	Where
long, long ago	in an enchanted castle
yesterday	on the playground
during the time of the dinosaurs	aboard the space shuttle
during the ice age	on Venus
at midnight	inside a volcano

45. WISH YOU WERE HERE!

Have your students design a postcard. Ask them to pretend they are on an imaginary vacation any-where in the universe. For example, they could be on top of Mount Everest, inside a cave at the bottom of the Pacific Ocean, or on a shuttle flight to see the rings of Saturn. Have them write a postcard describing their vacation to a friend or relative. Students can draw a picture of their location on the back of the postcard.

46. SHE SHOOTS! SHE SCORES!

Use gym class as inspiration for writing sports stories. After an exciting game of soccer, floor hockey, or other favorite sport, have the students write a sports commentary describing the game. Encourage them to use plenty of action verbs and colorful descriptions. Share the stories during "Sports Report": students sit at a desk with a "microphone" and read their stories in their best sports' announcer voice. If possible, videotape the presentations, then let the students each take the videotape home for one night to watch themselves on TV.

47. FIELD TRIP FEVER

Students are usually bubbling with excitement over field trips. Often, however, classes return at the end of the day, just in time to go home. Have your students write about a field trip for homework or first thing the next day. Ask the students to write a newspaper article about the trip, remembering to include the five Ws—who, what, where, when, and why. Or have them describe the trip in a letter to a friend or relative.

48. WHAT'S A *WHATSIT*?

Brainstorm a list of animals. Have the students choose any two animals from the list or think of two of their own. Combine the two animals to form a *whatsit*. For example, a frog combined with a grasshopper might be called a *froghopper*. Have them write a story about this strange, new animal. Ask them to describe what it looks like, where it lives, what it eats, and any unusual habits it may have. When the stories are complete, the students can draw their creatures.

toad	buffalo	camel
butterfly	hyena	crocodile
owl	grasshopper	elephant
zebra	moose	polar bear
frog	pelican	tiger

SUGGESTED READING

The Whingdingdilly by Bill Peet

The Mixed-Up Chameleon by Eric Carle

The Muddledy Fuddledy Mixed-Up Day by Janet Slater Redhead

49. THE MAGIC POTION

Bring a glass or beaker of colored water into the classroom. Add a few drops of vanilla or peppermint extract. Ask the students to pretend that it is a magic potion you have concocted in the science lab. Have them describe its color and smell, then write a story about what might happen if someone accidently spilled the magic potion. Remind the students to include a "recipe" to make their own magic potion.

50. ANIMAL ADVENTURES

Try these story titles when studying an animal theme.

- The Cuddly Porcupine
- The Camel with Five Humps
- The Flying Frog
- An Octopus Hug
- Inside My Cocoon
- The Talking Dolphin
- The Elephant That Could Dance
- The Spider That Spinned Golden Thread
- The Fish That Was Afraid of Water
- The Worm That Could Write

51. TALL TALES

Read *Pecos Bill,* the story of the legendary cowboy, or *Paul Bunyan,* the adventures of the larger-than-life lumberjack, both retold by Steven Kellogg. Invite the students to write another tall-tale adventure for one of these heroes or invent a character of their own to write about. Before writing, have the students create a character web for their hero and his or her unusual abilities. Remind students that tall-tale characters have exaggerated strengths, but not magical powers. Have them fill their stories with "whoppers"!

Whoppers

one day I went fishing and caught a long tailed shark. It took me 2 days to get it in the boat. But finally I got it in the boat. It was 100 feet long. so I brought it home. it took me and my family a month to eat all of it. the End

"Whoppers" by Cedar, age 8

52. WHODUNIT?

Try this activity during a mystery theme. Bring a bag or box of small, unrelated items to the classroom—a key, a small mirror, coins, a store receipt, and so on. Instruct the students that these items are clues found at the scene of a crime. You can outline the crime for them or make up one together. For example, a famous painting was stolen from an art gallery, or a top-secret formula is missing from a laboratory. You may wish to include other details (for example, "a man wearing a large black hat was seen leaving the scene of the crime"). Have the students create a story web to organize the clues before solving the mystery. They may add as many characters as they like and invent a detective to work on the case.

SUGGESTED READING

Stories from the Encyclopedia Brown series by Donald J. Sobol

Flatfoot Fox and the Case of the Missing Eye by Eth Clifford

Mystery of the Missing Fuzzy by Ski Michaels

Nate the Great by Marjorie Weinman Sharmat

53. THANK YOU, SANTA

Read *Thank You, Santa* by Margaret Wild. In this
Australian story, Samantha and Santa become pen
pals after Samantha sends Santa a thank-you note.
Each month they exchange letters. After reading the
story, have each student write Samantha's reply to
Santa's last letter or write a letter of their own to
Santa. Perhaps older students could write Santa's
reply.

54. CONVERSATIONS

Have the students write a dialogue between

- the sun and the moon
- a flower and a bee
- a bird and a tree
- an umbrella and a raindrop
- a flag and the wind
- a monitor and a keyboard
- a glass and a straw
- a ball and a bat
- a pencil and paper
- the hands of a clock

The Sun and the Moon
Get in a Fight

One day the sun got in a fight with the moon. They both wanted to be up at day and night. The stars knew all about it and they were the ones to solve it. All the stars gathered around. They had a big meeting. They had an idea. They would make a big wall called the milky way for the moon. Then the stars phoned up the clouds. The stars said, "At night push the sun into the ground." The clouds said, "O.K." The next day and night the stars did their job and the clouds did their job.

That's why today the sun is only up at day, and the moon is up at night.
The End

"The Sun and the Moon Get in a Fight" by Tommy, age 7

55. STORY STARTERS II

Copy each of the following story starters onto a recipe file card. Use them to start a collection of story ideas. Store them in a recipe box with blank cards so students can add ideas of their own.

✐ A flash of blinding light lit up the night sky.

✐ I could see the black clouds swirling toward us.

✐ There sitting on the edge of the pond was...

✐ "Did you hear that?" I whispered.

✐ As I was hiking through the forest, I came upon...

✐ Once upon a time, there lived a beautiful princess who wanted to learn how to fly.

✐ The little old man slowly turned his head toward me.

✐ I looked around the classroom. I didn't recognize one face.

✐ The mysterious music was coming from...

✐ The silver disk hovered above my backyard.

✐ Suddenly I heard a voice.

ALIENS!
One day a silver disk
hovered above my back
yard. Suddenly I heard a
voice. I looked back I
said to myself ALIENS!
I blinked and it was gone.
I thought it was my
imagination but maybe
not and from then on I've
always remembred that.

"Aliens!" by Jan, age 8

56. FLOWER LEGENDS

Share Tomie dePaola's flower legends, *The Legend of the Indian Paintbrush* and *The Legend of the Bluebonnet*, with the students. Help them brainstorm a list of wildflowers indigenous to your region. Have them use the colors and the characteristics of one of the flowers to write a legend about how it came to be.

57. WHAT'S THE SCORE?

Bring different kinds of sports equipment into the classroom; for example, a tennis ball, hockey puck, baseball glove, and a skipping rope. Have the students brainstorm questions they would ask each piece of equipment if they were a sports reporter. Record the questions on the chalkboard or chart paper. Here are some samples.

Tennis ball

- How many games have you played?
- What is the fastest speed you have traveled?
- What is your favorite part of tennis?
- How does it feel when the racket hits you?

Baseball glove

- Describe the toughest catch you ever made.
- What do you do in the off-season?
- How does your owner look after you?
- What is your favorite position to play? Why?

Have each student choose one piece of equipment to write about, using the interview questions as a guide.

SUGGESTED READING

Jinx Glove by Matt Christopher

58. JUST PERFECT!

Read *Be a Perfect Person in Just Three Days*, Stephen Manes' humorous story about Milo Crinkley's quest for perfection. After reading the story, ask the students to outline a self-improvement plan like Dr. Silverfish's. Try these topics, or have students invent their own:

- Be a hockey hero in just...
- Be a rock star in just...
- Be a genius in just...
- Be a millionaire in just...
- Be a best-selling author in just...

59. MURPHY

Read *Murphy* by Tatiana Tonks to the students. In it, Murphy the cat has a knack of getting Patrick into trouble. Finally Patrick has had enough and refuses to listen to Murphy. Murphy decides to hang around with Patrick's dad instead and winds up getting him into trouble. After Patrick has a talk with his dad, Murphy knows he will have to find someone else to get into trouble—Mom! Ask the students to write a story about Murphy's adventures with Patrick's mom.

60. WHERE DOES IT COME FROM?

Ask the students to choose one object (for example, a wooden desk, a pencil, a piece of paper, an eraser, or a piece of chalk) from the classroom, and think about what the object is made of and where it came from. Have them pretend to be the object and write a story about their origin and how they finally ended up in the classroom.

SUGGESTED READING

Agatha's Feather Bed by Carmen Agra Deedy

61. ARE YOU LISTENING?

In *The Other Way to Listen,* Byrd Baylor invites the reader to connect with the natural world simply by being open to its possibilities. After reading the book to your students, ask them to choose a small natural item such as a seed, rock, pine cone, or small plant. Ask them to listen to the object for a few minutes and then write down whatever message it conveys. Ask them: Does the object sing or murmur? Does it speak or laugh? What does it say to you?

62. MY WORST DAY EVER!

Read *A Difficult Day* by Eugenie Fernandes to the students. Then ask them to think of a day when everything went wrong. Share some of your bad days, too. Have the students write a story about their worst day, either real or imagined, and ask them to tell if everything worked out all right by the end of the day. Students might also like to write about their best day ever.

SUGGESTED READING

Alexander and the Terrible, Horrible, No Good, Very Bad Day by Judith Viorst

The Wrong Side of Bed

Today I woke up on the wrong side of bed
I walked to my closet, where I bumped my
head
I went roller-skating and hit a bump
Well that really hurt my rump
I thought that I'd go up to my old
tree-house
And I heard a SQUEEK! and it was a
mouse
That mouse scared me so
That day I found out how fast I
could go
Today I woke up on the wrong side of
bed,
Boy I hate that big fat bump on
my head!

"The Wrong Side of the Bed" by Paul, age 9

63. A CLEAN SWEEP

Enlist your caretaker's help for this activity. Borrow a variety of different brooms and mops from your school caretaker. Ask the students to think of stories they have read in which brooms figured prominently. Ask them: How did the broom behave? Was it cooperative? Did it work hard? Could it speak? Have each student "adopt" one of the caretaker's brooms and write a story about a day in its life.

SUGGESTED READING

The Widow's Broom by Chris Van Allsburg

Tsugele's Broom by Valerie Scho Carey

64. MY BEST FRIEND

Ask the students to think about their best friends. What makes someone a best friend? How do best friends treat each other? What do best friends do together? What happens if best friends disagree or fight? Have each student write a story about his or her best friend, telling about a happy time they spent together or about a quarrel they had.

SUGGESTED READING

The Rat and the Tiger by Keiko Kasza

Franklin Is Bossy by Paulette Bourgeois

65. ALL ABOUT ME

Early in the school year, many primary teachers like to use an "All About Me" theme to help them get to know their students and to build children's self-esteem. Have your students use the following story starters to make an "All About Me" book.

- I like to...
- When I grow up...
- I would like to learn how to...
- I love to give...
- I sometimes get angry when...
- The funniest thing that ever happened to me was...
- I love to eat...
- At school I like to...
- I'm good at...
- My family likes to...

66. LITTLE PEOPLE

Ask your students: What would you do if you discovered a basket of tiny people in your backyard? What kind of home would you build them? What could they use for furniture? How would you feed them? Write a story about the little people who come to live with you.

SUGGESTED READING

The Rainbabies by Laura Krauss Melmed

Little Fingerling by Monica Hughes

The Littles to the Rescue by John Peterson

The Littles and Their Friends by John Peterson

Thumbelina by Hans Christian Andersen

Thumbelina, retold by Deborah Hautzig

67. THE CHITCHAT

Once a year, Danny the Drifter drops in for a cup of tea and a chitchat with his sister, the respectable widow Mrs. Gimble. After reading *The Three-Legged Cat* by Margaret Mahy, ask the students to write about the chitchat Danny and his sister will have next year when he returns from a year of roaming the world with her cat.

68. BE CAREFUL WHAT YOU WISH FOR

"Be careful what you wish for, you might just get it." Ask the students if they have heard this saying before and what they think it means. Brainstorm a list of wishes the students have had that they really didn't want to come true. For example:

- I wish my little brother would run away from home.

- I wish I never had to have a bath.

- I wish I could stay up as late as I want.

Have the students choose one wish and write a story about what would happen if the wish really did come true.

SUGGESTED READING

The Fisherman and His Wife by the Brothers Grimm

A Little Excitement by Marc Harshman

69. *POURQUOI* STORIES

Rudyard Kipling's *Just So Stories* provide an explanation of many natural occurrences. After reading some of these to the students, ask them to write a *pourquoi* story. Have them choose a topic from the list below or make up one of their own.

why bees buzz	why tigers are striped
why clouds float	why the wind blows
why hyenas laugh	why dogs have tails
why birds fly	why porcupines have quills
why cows moo	why the rhinoceros has one horn
why horses gallop	why zebras are black and white

SUGGESTED READING

Anansi the Spider by Gerald McDermott

Why Mosquitoes Buzz in People's Ears by Verna Aardema

How the Birds Got Wings

Once the birds were little things crawling on the ground. They looked like birds with tails but no wings.

One day the birds were getting few and had many close escapes. The king decided to go to Mother Nature to ask for help. The journey was going to be dangerous but they had to do it. So they set out to her palace.

On the way they met up with a great big snake. The snake said, "I'll eat you up if you don't give me one of your feathers!" The birds each gave up one of their beautiful feathers for the snake and kept on walking.

When they were finally half way they met a foolish fox called Sarah. Sarah said " I am the best! I can walk to the lake." She stuck her nose in the air and walked right into a tree. She fell down.

The birds kept on walking.

They finally got there and they said, "Mother Nature strong and true please give us wings, make us fly all together or we might die." Mother Nature came down. She said, "Little bird you have come here for nothing, unless you give up something you already have." The smallest bird said, "We could give away our tails." "Give away our tails!" said two shocked Jays. "Yes," said the king "it's the only way." "Fine," said Mother Nature. (And thats how the birds got wings. Birds who can't fly took a different chance.) The End

"How the Birds Got Wings" by Jennifer, age 8

70. WRITING LAUNCH PADS

Write the following list on the chalkboard or chart paper:

trees	weather	grandparents
parks	skating	boats
music	skiing	computers
fireworks	beach	rain
sister	sleepovers	holidays
pets	toys	weiner roast
airplanes	bikes	soccer

Tell your students: Choose one word that reminds you of something or of an experience you have had. Turn your memories into a story.

Add to the list throughout the school year and keep it posted at your writing center.

71. FAMILY TRADITIONS

Share some of your family traditions with the students and ask the students to share some of theirs. Record these on chart paper by occasion: Christmas, Thanksgiving, Hanukkah, birthdays, and so on. Ask the students to choose their favorite family tradition and write about it.

SUGGESTED READING

Night Tree by Eve Bunting

72. TRAVELING STORIES

Fill a small, old suitcase with a variety of paper, pens, pencils, and other assorted writing tools. Include a couple of good travel storybooks such as *Grandfather's Journey* by Allen Say or *Travels for Two* by Stephane Poulin. Allow each child to take the suitcase home for a night. After reading the books, invite each child to write a story about a real or imaginary trip that he or she has taken. Keep these stories in a storage box in the classroom. When all the children have written something, replace the storybooks with their short stories. Then let them take the suitcase home a second time, so everyone gets an opportunity to read what their classmates' have written.

73. MEANWHILE…

Read *Meanwhile Back at the Ranch* by Trinka Hakes Noble to your students. This hilarious book tells the story of Rancher Hicks and his wife Elna who lead boring lives until the day the rancher heads into town. Have the students write their own version of the story. Some possible titles are:

- Meanwhile Back at My House
- Meanwhile Back in My Room
- Meanwhile Back at My Birthday Party
- Meanwhile Back in the Classroom

74. THE PERFECT NAME

Have students find out how they were named. You might send home a questionnaire for parents to complete, asking:

- How did you choose your child's name?
- Was your child named after someone?
- Does your child's name have special meaning?
- What other names were you considering for your child?

When students have collected the information, have them write a story about how they were named.

SUGGESTED READING

Chrysanthemum by Kevin Henkes
Laura Charlotte by Kathryn O. Galbraith

75. PIPE DOWN!

"Speak softly, please." "Use your inside voices." "Just whisper to each other." "Please adjust the volume." Teachers continually remind their exuberant students to keep their voices down. In *Effie* by Beverley Allinson and *A Very Noisy Girl* by Elizabeth Winthrop, having a loud voice can be an advantage. Read one or both of the stories to the students, then ask them to write about a time when a loud voice came in handy.

76. STORY ENDINGS I

Instead of giving students the opening sentence to a story, give them an ending instead. Some suggestions are:

- The strange noise stopped as suddenly as it had started.

- I watched the silver spaceship lift off and disappear into the night sky.

- I knew that we would be best friends forever.

- It was the best birthday I had ever had.

- I am the luckiest person in the world!

- I was safe at last.

- There before us stood the treasure we had been searching for.

- "Thank you," said the giant as he stepped over the hillside.

- The fire was out and finally we could rest.

- In the morning I realized it was only a dream.

77. PROVE IT!

Write several statements on the chalkboard or chart paper. For example:

✎ Vanilla ice cream is the best.

✎ Three out of every four people prefer vanilla ice cream.

✎ My soccer team is better than yours.

✎ My soccer team won the city championship.

Ask the students to identify which statements are fact and which are opinions. Tell them that facts are necessary to convince someone or to win an argument. Have the students write a paragraph about one of the following topics or one of their own choosing. First have them make a list of facts that will support the argument they are going to make.

✎ Every child should get five [ten, twenty] dollars a week for allowance.

✎ It would be fun [horrible] to be a teacher.

✎ Every kid should have an exotic pet.

✎ I need a new bike [pair of runners, ball, glove].

✎ Sleepovers are fun.

78. THE TOMORROW STONE

In *The Yesterday Stone* by Peter Eyvindson, Anna's grandmother cherishes and shares the stories evoked by her special stone. Read the story to the students and then ask them to find a special stone and bring it to school. When they have brought their stones to school, ask the students to rub and polish the stones the way Anna and her grandmother do until the stone is warm enough to tell a story about the future. Then have them write down what the stone is telling them.

SUGGESTED READING

The Wretched Stone by Chris Van Allsburg

79. THE AMAZING BONE

Read *The Amazing Bone* by William Steig. Pearl, the pig, finds a most unusual bone on her way home from school. Not only can it talk, but it also outsmarts highway robbers and a fox. Have the students be on the lookout for something unusual on their way home from school, such as a rock, a feather, a leaf, or a pine cone. When the students bring their objects to school, have them pretend their objects can talk. Ask them to write a conversation with the object or have them write about an adventure the object has had.

80. THE HELPFUL GIANT

Big Jeremy by Steven Kroll tells the story of a lovable and helpful giant who lives at the edge of an apple orchard. Jeremy helps the owners of the orchard by plowing the fields, picking the apples, repairing the buildings, and playing with the grandchildren. After reading the story ask the students to write a story about a giant who comes to live with them. How could he help? What would he eat? Where would he sleep? What games could they play with a giant? What would he look like?

81. NICE TO MEET YOU!

Have each student think of a favorite story character. Tell them that for this writing activity they will have to pretend to be the character. Then divide the students into pairs. Have the students introduce themselves to each other in writing only and carry on a written conversation. For example:

STUDENT 1: Hi! My name is Goldilocks. I've just had a terrible fright!

STUDENT 2: Nice to meet you, Goldilocks. My name is Rumpelstiltskin, but please don't tell anyone. I'm trying to keep it a secret. What frightened you?

82. THE MAGIC PEARL

Purchase an inexpensive imitation pearl necklace and give each student one "pearl" from it. Explain that it is a magic pearl that can increase anything it is placed on. For example, if the pearl is placed on a book, soon there will be one hundred books. If it is placed in a crayon box, soon the box will be overflowing with crayons. Ask the students to write a story about how they will use their magic pearl.

SUGGESTED READING

The Dragon's Pearl by Julie Lawson

83. ANOTHER BUSY DAY FOR A GOOD GRANDMOTHER

Mrs. Oberon, a very busy and modern grandmother, travels by trail bike, raft, airplane, and skateboard to deliver a special cake to her son. Encounters with avalanches, alligators, and vultures are easily taken in stride by the feisty Mrs. Oberon in Margaret Mahy's *A Busy Day for a Good Grandmother*. After reading the story to the students ask them to write about another busy day for the good grandmother. What might happen if her son loses the cake recipe?

84. MY DREAM VACATION

Tell the students that they are going to have a chance to plan the vacation of a lifetime. To help them plan it, first have them answer the following questions:

- Where will you go?
- How will you travel?
- Who will travel with you?
- How long will you be gone?
- Where will you stay?
- What will you bring home with you?

After they have written about their dream vacation, have the students design a T-shirt that can become the cover of their published story.

85. JUST FOR A DAY

In her Just for a Day series of wildlife books, Joanne Ryder invites readers to spend a day as a polar bear, a Canada goose, a humpback whale, a sea otter, or a lizard. After sharing the books with the students, ask them to choose an animal that they would like to be for a day. After researching their animals' homes, food, habitat, and habits, have them write a story about one day in their life as that animal.

86. THE MONEY JAR

Share with students a time when you saved up for a special purchase. Ask them to share similar stories. Ask them: What were you saving up for? Were you saving to buy yourself something or was it a gift for someone else? Did you keep the money in a jar or special container? How long did it take to save up enough money? Did you have to give up something else to save for the special item? Have the students write about it. When they are finished, read *A Chair for My Mother* by Vera B. Williams.

87. PRINCESS FROWNSALOT

Princess Frownsalot frowns so much that her face gets stuck in a frown. There is only one solution—a smile transplant! After reading *Princess Frownsalot* by John Bianchi to the students, ask them to think of a body part that they would like to exchange and write a story about it. Some titles might be:

- Prince Brushcut
- Princess Long Legs
- Prince Singsalot
- Princess Green Eyes
- Prince Talksalittle
- Princess High Jumper

88. WE'RE IN THIS TOGETHER!

Give each cooperative-learning group five minutes to brainstorm the first sentence for a story. When the time is up, ask one student in each group to record the sentence on a piece of paper or in a group journal. Then, without speaking, the student passes the paper or journal to the next student in the group who writes the next sentence of the story. Have each group member take a turn writing a sentence until a story is completed.

89. THE FIRST DOG

In *The First Dog* by Jan Brett, Kip the cave boy befriends a Paleowolf and names him Dog, "one who wags his tail." When the story ends, Kip is bringing the first dog home to his family. After reading the story, ask the students to write about an adventure that Kip and Dog have. Use Jan Brett's illustrations of Pleistocene animals for story ideas.

- the mammoth hunt
- the lost cave bear cubs
- attack of the wooly rhino
- the injured saber-toothed cat

90. MY FAVORITES

Have the students choose a topic below or think of one of their own favorite things. Encourage them to write about why it is and how it became their favorite.

my favorite color	my favorite food
my favorite animal	my favorite TV show
my favorite book	my favorite movie
my favorite season	my favorite time of day
my favorite place	my favorite holiday

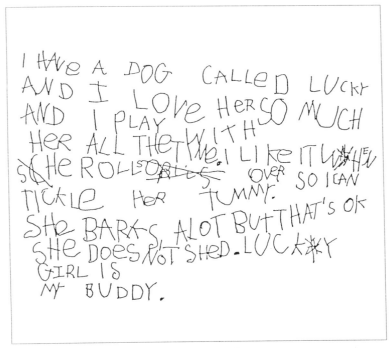

"My Favorite Pet" by Kathryn Ann, age 6

91. LET'S PLAY!

This cooperative group writing activity will take several days to complete. Read a fairy tale to the students and then together rewrite the story as a play. Show students the correct format for a script and how to lift dialogue out of the story, and explain the role of a narrator. Then help each cooperative group choose a simple fairy tale to re-write as a play. Look for stories with three or four characters, one or two settings, and a simple plot. When the plays are complete, invite the groups to perform them for each other or another class, or have them make puppets and put on a puppet show.

92. THE SNOW SPEAKS

Read *The Snow Speaks* by Nancy White Carlstrom. From the first snowfall of the season to the firm, sure crust of deep winter, the snow speaks to those who know how to listen. After reading the story to the students ask them to choose a topic from the list below or make up one of their own to write about.

the rain whispers	the thunder roars
the hail hammers	the trees sigh
the stream laughs	the waves shout

93. A PUZZLING STORY

Use cooperative groups for this story idea. Give each group several pieces from a jigsaw puzzle. Ask each group to write a story based on the puzzle pieces. Who are the characters? What is the setting? What problem could they solve? How will they solve it? After each group has shared its story, let the students fit all the puzzle pieces together to discover what the finished jigsaw looks like. Some groups might like to write another story about the completed jigsaw puzzle.

SUGGESTED READING

The Last Piece of Sky by Tim Wynne-Jones

94. SEASONAL VISITORS

What if each season was actually a person? What would Spring look like? Would Autumn be a girl or a boy? How would Winter speak? What would Summer wear? Ask the students to choose one season and imagine what it would be like, then write a story about the day their seasonal visitor arrived.

SUGGESTED READING

The Stranger by Chris Van Allsburg

Good-bye Geese by Nancy White Carlstrom

95. GOING BUGGY

Take advantage of young students' fascination with bugs. Have each of your cooperative-learning groups capture an insect during recess or after school. Tell the students to look for ants, ladybugs, crickets, or beetles. Help each group make a temporary home in a glass jar for its insect. When all the groups have an insect, give each a magnifying glass, and have them observe their insect in its jar. Assign one question to each person in the group.

- What does your insect look like?
- How does your insect move?
- What do you think your insect would feel like?
- How does your insect eat?

Using the questions as a guide, have each group write a story about its insect.

Read *Sam's Sandwich* by David Pelham, *"Leave That Cricket Be, Alan Lee"* by Barbara Ann Porte, and *Two Bad Ants* by Chris Van Allsburg, then have each group release its insect.

96. THE DOG WHO HAD KITTENS

In *The Dog Who Had Kittens* by Polly M. Robertus, Baxter the bassett hound helps Eloise the cat care for her new kittens. After reading the story to the students, ask them to imagine what it would be like if a dog really had kittens. What if a cow had piglets? What if a horse had puppies? Have them write about a mixed-up animal family!

97. STORY GRAMMAR

A story grammar is a summary of the main events, settings, and characters in a story. Students who understand the structure of a story are better able to identify important ideas. Choose a familiar story, such as a fairy tale, to read to the class. When finished, display a simple story grammar on the chalkboard or chart paper—make three boxes and label them *beginning, middle,* and *end.* Ask students to recall the story and determine where important story events happened. Record the events under the correct heading. Once students can identify a basic story structure, add elements such as:

- settings
- characters
- problems that arise
- how problems are solved

98. WRITING BUDDIES

If the students in your class are twinned with older students in your school as reading buddies or care partners, have them try some of the following writing activities:

- write and exchange letters with their older buddies
- work as partners with their buddies to create big books for the school's kindergarten class
- dictate their stories to their buddies
- write letters to Santa

If the students in your class are twinned with younger students in your school as reading buddies or care partners, have them try some of the following writing activities:

- write and exchange letters with their younger buddies
- work with their younger buddies to create big books for the school's kindergarten class
- edit their buddies' stories
- write and illustrate a book all about their little buddy, then read the story together
- answer their buddies' letters to Santa

99. BEGINNING, MIDDLE, AND END

This cooperative jigsaw activity is designed to reinforce the concept of story structure learned by completing a story grammar (see page 81). Divide the students into groups of three. Assign each group member beginning, middle, or end.

Have all the beginning group members meet in one area of the classroom, all the middle group members meet in another area, and all the end group members meet in a third area. Ask them to talk about what they think should happen in their part of a story. Assign one person to record the group's findings. For example:

Beginning	Middle	End
◆ the opening sentence should grab the reader's attention ◆ characters are introduced ◆ setting is described	◆ a problem arises ◆ characters are developed ◆ the setting may change	◆ the problem is solved ◆ the characters learn something ◆ the setting may change

When the "expert" groups have finished discussing their part of the story, have them return to their home groups and share what they have learned. Then have each group of three outline a story that has a distinct beginning, middle, and end. Each group member can be responsible for writing the part of the story that he or she was assigned.

100. MY TEACHER, THE WRITER

Model writing by participating in writing activities yourself. It shows students how much you value writing and helps you understand the difficulties writers sometimes encounter. Keep a journal and let students take turns editing your work. Ask them to give you suggestions for improving your writing. From time to time, share your revised pieces with them and celebrate the joy of writing!

Appendix

THE WRITING PROCESS: SKILLS CHECKLIST

student's name	date	

	Often	Sometimes	Seldom
1. PREWRITING			
Initiates writing independently	❏	❏	❏
Chooses a variety of topics	❏	❏	❏
Writes for a variety of purposes	❏	❏	❏
Writes for a variety of audiences	❏	❏	❏
Chooses formats appropriate to audience and purpose	❏	❏	❏
2. DRAFTING			
Takes risks by using invented spelling	❏	❏	❏
Expresses ideas in sentences	❏	❏	❏
Incorporates own experiences and knowledge	❏	❏	❏
Orders ideas in logical and interesting ways	❏	❏	❏
Enhances writing by using descriptive words, phrases, and images	❏	❏	❏
3. REVISING AND EDITING			
Proofreads for clarity of meaning	❏	❏	❏
Proofreads for accurate capitalization	❏	❏	❏
Proofreads for accurate punctuation	❏	❏	❏
Proofreads for accurate spelling	❏	❏	❏
Incorporates responses and suggestions of others in revisions	❏	❏	❏
Expands writing by adding details and/or examples	❏	❏	❏
Deletes unnecessary information	❏	❏	❏
4. PUBLISHING			
Final draft is written neatly and legibly	❏	❏	❏
Can evaluate effectiveness of own writing	❏	❏	❏
Willing to share final drafts through reading, display, and/or performance	❏	❏	❏

(Adapted from the Saskatchewan K-5 Language Arts Curriculum, June 1992)

EVALUATING WRITING SAMPLES: RATING SCALE 1–5

_____   _____
student's name   date

(5) · · · · · · · · · · · · · (3) · · · · · · · · · · · · · (1)

5	3	1
☐ There is an obvious beginning, middle, and ending.	☐ Beginning, middle, and ending are somewhat defined.	☐ Beginning, middle, and ending are poorly defined.
☐ Character development is strong.	☐ Character development is satisfactory.	☐ Character development is weak.
☐ Setting is well established.	☐ Setting is somewhat established.	☐ Setting is not established.
☐ Plot is well developed.	☐ Plot is somewhat developed.	☐ Plot is poorly developed.
☐ Sentence structure is varied.	☐ Sentence structure is somewhat varied.	☐ No sentence structure variety.
☐ High-frequency words are usually spelled correctly.	☐ High-frequency words are occasionally spelled correctly.	☐ High-frequency words are rarely spelled correctly.
☐ Uses readable invented spelling for low-frequency words.	☐ Occasionally uses invented spelling for low-frequency words.	☐ Rarely uses invented spelling for low-frequency words.
☐ Consistent and proper use of capitalization.	☐ Occasionally uses proper capitalization.	☐ Seldom uses proper capitalization.
☐ Consistent and proper use of punctuation.	☐ Occasionally uses proper punctuation.	☐ Seldom uses proper punctuation.
☐ Final drafts are neat and legible.	☐ Final drafts are occasionally neat and legible.	☐ Final drafts are seldom neat and legible.

CONFERENCE RECORD

_____   _____
                student's name   date

Topic/Title: _____

_____

_____

Strengths: _____

_____

_____

Needs to Work On: _____

_____

_____

Spelling Words: _____

_____

_____

Teacher's Comments: _____

_____

_____

Student's Comments: _____

_____

_____

CHILDREN'S LITERATURE

Aardema, Verna. *Why Mosquitoes Buzz in People's Ears.* New York: Dial Press, 1975.

Alexander, Lloyd. *The Fortune-Tellers.* New York: Dutton Children's Books, 1992.

Allinson, Beverley. *Effie.* Toronto: Summerhill Press, 1990.

Andersen, Hans Christian. *Thumbelina.* London: Dent, 1979.

Andersen, Hans Christian. *Thumbelina.* Retold by Deborah Hautzig. New York: Knopf, 1990.

Baker, Keith. *The Magic Fan.* San Diego: Harcourt Brace Jovanovich, 1989.

Baker, Leslie. *The Antique Store Cat.* Boston: Little, Brown, 1992.

————. *The Third-Story Cat.* Boston: Little, Brown, 1987.

Barkan, Joanne. *Anna Marie's Blanket.* New York: Barron's, 1990.

Baylor, Byrd. *The Other Way to Listen.* New York: Scribner, 1978.

————. *Everybody Needs a Rock.* New York: C. Scribner's Sons, 1974.

Bianchi, John. *Princess Frownsalot.* Newburgh, ON: Bungalo Books, 1987.

Bourgeois, Paulette. *Franklin Is Bossy.* Toronto: Kids Can Press, 1993.

Brett, Jan. *The Mitten.* New York: Putnam, 1989.

————. *The First Dog.* San Diego: Harcourt Brace Jovanovich, 1988.

Brothers Grimm. *The Fisherman and His Wife*. Mankato, MN: Creative Education, 1983.

Bunting, Eve. *Night Tree.* San Diego: Harcourt Brace Jovanovich, 1991.

Calmenson, Stephanie. *The Principal's New Clothes.* New York: Scholastic, 1989.

Carey, Valerie Scho. *Tsugele's Broom.* New York: HarperCollins, 1993.

Carle, Eric. *The Mixed-Up Chameleon.* New York: Crowell, 1975.

Carlstrom, Nancy White. *The Snow Speaks.* Boston: Little, Brown, 1992.

———. *Good-bye Geese.* New York: Philomel Books, 1991.

Carrick, Carol. *Aladdin and the Wonderful Lamp.* New York: Scholastic, 1989.

Christopher, Matt. *Jinx Glove.* Boston: Little, Brown, 1974.

Clifford, Eth. *Flatfoot Fox and the Case of the Missing Eye.* Boston: Houghton Mifflin, 1990.

Clifton, Lucille. *Three Wishes.* New York: Delacorte Press, 1992.

Cummings, Pat. *Clean Your Room, Harvey Moon!* New York: Bradbury Press, 1991.

Deedy, Carmen Agra. *Agatha's Feather Bed.* Atlanta: Peachtree, 1991.

Demi. *Liang and the Magic Paintbrush.* New York: Holt, Rinehard & Winston, 1988.

De Paola, Tomie. *The Legend of the Indian Paintbrush.* New York: Putnam, 1988.

———. *The Legend of the Bluebonnet.* New York: Putnam, 1983.

———. *Big Anthony and the Magic Ring.* New York: Harcourt Brace Jovanovich, 1979.

———. *Strega Nona.* Englewood Cliffs, NJ: Prentice-Hall, 1975.

Duncan, Frances. *The Toothpaste Genie.* Richmond Hill, ON: Scholastic-TAB, 1981.

Eyvindson, Peter. *The Yesterday Stone.* Winnipeg, MB: Pemmican, 1992.

Fernandes, Eugenie. *A Difficult Day.* Toronto: Kids Can Press, 1987.

Flournoy, Valerie. *The Patchwork Quilt.* New York: Dial Books for Young Readers, 1985.

Galbraith, Kathryn O. *Laura Charlotte*. New York: Philomel, 1990.

Garrett, Jennifer. *The Queen Who Stole the Sky*. Richmond Hill, ON: North Winds Press, 1986.

Gilman, Phoebe. *Something From Nothing*. Richmond Hill, ON: North Winds Press, 1992.

———. *The Balloon Tree*. Richmond Hill, ON: North Winds Press, 1984.

Goennel, Heidi. *If I Were a Penguin*. Boston: Little, Brown, 1989.

Harshman, Marc. *A Little Excitement*. New York: Cobblehill Books, E.P. Dutton, 1989.

Henkes, Kevin. *Chrysanthemum*. New York: Greenwillow, 1991.

Hest, Amy. *The Purple Coat*. New York: Four Winds Press, 1986.

Hillman, Elizabeth. *Min-Yo and the Moon Dragon*. San Diego: Harcourt Brace Jovanovich, 1992.

Hughes, Monica. *Little Fingerling*. Toronto: Kids Can Press, 1989.

Hutchins, Pat. *The Very Worst Monster*. New York: Greenwillow, 1985.

Kasza, Keiko. *The Rat and the Tiger*. New York: G.P. Putnam's Sons, 1993.

———. *The Wolf's Chicken Stew*. New York: Putnam, 1987.

Kellogg, Steven. *Pecos Bill*. New York: Morrow, 1986.

———. *Paul Bunyan*. New York: Morrow, 1984.

Kipling, Rudyard. *Just So Stories*. New York: Knopf, 1986.

Kroll, Steven. *Big Jeremy*. New York: Holiday House, 1989.

Lawson, Julie. *The Dragon's Pearl*. Toronto: Oxford University Press, 1992.

Lunn, Janet. *Amos's Sweater*. Vancouver, Toronto: Douglas & McIntyre, 1988.

Mahy, Margaret. *The Three-Legged Cat*. New York: Viking, 1993.

———. *A Busy Day for a Good Grandmother*. New York: Margaret K. McElderry Books, 1993.

Manes, Stephen. *Be a Perfect Person in Just Three Days*. New York: Clarion, 1982.

McDermott, Gerald. *Anansi the Spider*. New York: Holt, Rinehard & Winston, 1972.

Melmed, Laura Krauss. *The Rainbabies*. New York: Lothrop, Lee & Shepard, 1992.

Michaels, Ski. *Mystery of the Missing Fuzzy*. Mahwah, NJ: Troll Associates, 1986.

Muller, Robin. *The Magic Paintbrush*. Toronto: Doubleday Canada, 1989.

Munsch, Robert. *Thomas' Snowsuit*. Toronto: Annick Press, 1985.

————. *The Paper Bag Princess*. Toronto: Annick Press, 1980.

Noble, Trinka Hakes. *Meanwhile Back at the Ranch*. New York: Dial Books for Young Readers, 1987.

O'Neill, Mary Le Duc. *Hailstones and Halibut Bones*. New York: Doubleday, 1989.

Peet, Bill. *The Whingdingdilly*. Boston: Houghton Mifflin, 1970.

Pelham, David. *Sam's Sandwich*. New York: Dutton Children's Books, 1991.

Peterson, John. *The Littles and Their Friends*. New York: Scholastic, 1979.

————. *The Littles to the Rescue*. New York: Scholastic, 1968.

Polacco, Patricia. *The Keeping Quilt*. New York: Simon & Schuster, 1988.

Porte, Barbara Ann. *"Leave That Cricket Be, Alan Lee."* New York: Greenwillow, 1993.

Poulin, Stephane. *Travels for Two*. Toronto: Annick Press, 1991.

Redhead, Janet Slater. *The Muddledy Fuddledy Mixed-Up Day*. Austin, TX: Steck-Vaughn, 1990.

Robertus, Polly M. *The Dog Who Had Kittens*. New York: Holiday House, 1991.

Rockwell, Thomas. *How to Eat Fried Worms*. New York: F. Watts, 1973.

Ryder, Joanne. *Hello, Tree!* New York: Lodestar Books, 1991.

———. Just for a Day series. New York: Morrow Junior Books.

Say, Allen. *Grandfather's Journey*. Boston: Houghton Mifflin, 1993.

Scieszka, Jon. *The Frog Prince, Continued*. New York: Viking, 1991.

———. *The True Story of the Three Little Pigs*. New York: Viking, 1989.

Sharmat, Marjorie Weinman. *Nate the Great*. New York: Coward, McCann & Geoghegan, 1972.

Silverstein, Shel. *The Giving Tree*. New York: Harper & Row, 1964.

Simmie, Lois. *What Holds Up the Moon?* Regina, SK: Coteau Books, 1987.

Sobol, Donald J. Encyclopedia Brown series. Toronto: Bantam.

Steig, William. *The Amazing Bone*. New York: Farrar, Straus & Giroux, 1976.

Stewig, John. *Stone Soup*. New York: Holiday House, 1991.

Tonks, Tatiana. *Murphy*. Richmond Hill, ON: Scholastic, 1992.

Van Allsburg, Chris. *The Widow's Broom*. Boston: Houghton Mifflin, 1992.

———. *The Wretched Stone*. Boston: Houghton Mifflin, 1991.

———. *Two Bad Ants*. Boston: Houghton Mifflin, 1988.

———. *The Stranger*. Boston: Houghton Mifflin, 1986.

———. *The Wreck of the Zephyr*. Boston: Houghton Mifflin, 1983.

———. *The Sweetest Fig*. Boston: Houghton Mifflin, 1983.

Viorst, Judith. *Alexander and the Terrible, Horrible, No Good, Very Bad Day*. New York: Atheneum, 1972.

Wiesner, David. *June 29, 1999*. New York: Clarion Books, 1992.

———. *Hurricane*. New York: Clarion Books, 1990.

Wild, Margaret. *Thank You, Santa.* New York: Scholastic, 1991.

Williams, Jay. *Everyone Knows What a Dragon Looks Like.* New York: Four Winds Press, 1976.

Williams, Vera B. *A Chair for My Mother.* New York: Greenwillow, 1982.

Winthrop, Elizabeth. *A Very Noisy Girl.* New York: Holiday House, 1991.

Wynne-Jones, Tim. *The Last Piece of Sky.* Toronto: Douglas & McIntyre, 1993.

Bibliography

Atwell, Nancie. *In the Middle*. Portsmouth, NH: Heinemann, 1987.

Calkins, Lucy McCormick. *The Art of Teaching Writing*. Portsmouth, NH: Heinemann, 1986.

———. *Living Between the Lines*. Portsmouth, NH: Heinemann, 1991.

Cambourne, Brian. *The Whole Story*. Auckland, New Zealand: Ashton Scholastic, 1988.

Graves, Donald. *Writing: Teachers and Children at Work*. Portsmouth, NH: Heinemann, 1983.

Graves, Donald H., and Virginia Stuart. *Write from the Start: Tapping Your Child's Natural Writing Ability*. New York: Dutton, 1985.

Molyneux, Lynn. *Cooperative Learning, Writing and Success*. Canandaigua, NY: Trellis Books, 1991.

Parry, J., and D. Hornsby. *Write On: A Conference Approach to Writing.* Portsmouth, NH: Heinemann, 1988.

Saskatchewan English Language Arts Curriculum Guide. Saskatchewan Education, June, 1992.

The Learning Source. *Let's Write!* New York: Scholastic, 1993.

NOTES